WHEN THE BLACK LADY SINGS:

Musings of an African American Princess

S. Hafer Bronson

When the Black Lady Sings: Musings of an African American Princess

Copyright © 2016 S. Hafer Bronson
All rights reserved.

ISBN-10:0-9961327-2-4
ISBN-13:978-0-9961327-2-5

All rights reserved. Except for use in the case of brief quotations embodied in critical articles and reviews, the reproduction or utilization of this work in whole or part in any form by any electronic, digital, mechanical or other means, now known or hereafter invented, including xerography, photocopying, scanning, recording, or any information storage or retrieval system, is forbidden without prior written permission of the author and publisher.

The scanning, uploading, and distribution of this book via the Internet or via any other means without permission of the publisher and author is illegal and punishable by law. Purchase only authorized versions of this book and do not participate in or encourage electronic piracy of copyrighted materials. Your support of the author's rights is appreciated. Names, characters, places, and incidents are based on the author's own personal experience therefore names of persons and entities remain unnamed to protect the integrity of the story and the privacy of those involved. Any group or organization listed is for informational purposes only and does not imply endorsement or support of their activities or organization. For ordering, booking, permission, or questions, contact the author.

Published by Wryte Type Publishing, LLC

Cover Art & Design by Lloyd DeBerry, Fine Arts & Graphics
Printed in the United States of America

When the Black Lady Sings: Musings of an African American Princess

This book is dedicated to my
mother who carried me,
my father who raised me,
And to Him who
keeps me from falling.

S. Hafer Bronson

TABLE OF CONTENTS

<u>DESIRES</u>

In A Separate Place	13
The Weekend	14
Tumbled Linen	16
Don't Look in My Eyes	17
One Night in the Tropics	18
Let Me Put My Love on You	19
Solitude	20
Devotion	21
Work Wid Da Brotha	22
Intimacy	24
A Kiss Goodnight	25
Backdraft	26
The Moment	28
Insatiable Appetite	29
First Impressions	30
You Warm My Heart	31
Visions	32

EMPOWERMENT

Greatness	35
Storm	36
What Good Can Come of It?	37
Combination	38
Don't Underestimate Me	39
Pride	40
Abstract	42
The Betrayal	43
Widow's Peak	44
Everything's Cool	48
Drama	49
Gray	51
Forecast: Rain	52
Inner Visions	53

PASSAGES

Journey	57
The Touch	58
New Beginnings	62
In Remembrance Of....	63
Epic	64
An Understanding	66
Paces	67
Closed Doors	69
Endings	71
Farewell	72
In the Mourning	73
Honor	74
Did You Love Me, Ever?	75
Merging Lives	77
Final Notice	80

IDENTITY

Tyrone	83
Angelina	86
Billy	87
Identity	88
Ricki Lake	89
The Preacher	90
The Teacher	91
Sweet	93
Black Snake	95
Sonny Clark's Blues	97
Miss Helen	98
Nirka's Kitchen	99
The Art of Seduction	101
Walt	102
A Nun's Tale	103
Warmest Regards	105
Sister	106

Cousin, Mine	107
Panther	109
<u>MUSE (IC)</u>	
Theme from Taxi	113
The Music Lesson	114
Ode to a "Q"	115
Go Find You a Woman (Cause I sure as hell done found me a man)	116
Today I Bought a Pickup Truck	118
A Pledge of Love	121
My Momma Riding Shotgun	122
About the Author	125

Comfort   Consistency

NEED

Solitude   Intimacy

Contentment

Desire

Wholeness   Acceptance

WANT

Unity   Resolution

Passion   Peace

When the Black Lady Sings: Musings of an African American Princess

S. Hafer Bronson

In A Separate Place

In the still of the night,
In the midst of a storm,
I have no love to keep me warm.
The shelter I crave
The arms that embrace
Protect one who dwells
In a separate place.

While I struggle to reach
For the moments of bliss,
I can't help but recall
The formidable risk
Of engulfing my heart.
To one who must face,
Another, more tender,
In a separate place.

Loneliness is my companion
As I lay cross my bed.
With heightened awareness,
That it holds me instead.
I wrestle my loneliness
Night after night.
It squeezes me breathless,
And robs me of fight.
While sincerity guides you
As you continue to face,
A hug and a kiss
In a separate place.

The Weekend

There was something about that weekend.
She knew she had to go.
The message she received intrigued her.
Why? She did not know.

A new year was just emerging,
Her plans were incomplete.
Miss Get it Together, Miss Organized
Refused to accept defeat.

So this was something different,
Something to jumpstart her way.
This could be a time for reflection
Or a time for innocent play.

She packed her bags and departed,
Along with a confidante and friend.
They talked of their lives and expectations,
Of what they would find at journey's end.

As she walked into the building,
And saw him standing there,
She felt a sense of security,
That embraced her with loving care.

The weekend was beginning,
No doubts or wondering why.
Only thoughts of peace and serenity,
As she gazed into the midnight sky.

The chill of night air engulfed her
But its effect were barely felt.
For the more she looked upon him,
Her heart began to melt.

As day, then night, continued,
Their lives they did reveal.
But she would refuse to recognize
The intensity of what she'd feel.

The bond that was created
As they sat and talked of strife,
Would haunt them both long after
They parted to continue their lives.

The friendship between the two hearts,
A renewal of contentment of mind.
The feeling that no matter his choices,
She wanted him in her life.

So this had become the meeting,
That she wished would never end.
For as her Father had promised,
He had sent to her.....a friend.

Tumbled Linen

Until morning,
The scent of you lingers.
In the midst of my tumbled linen,
And saturates my body with your essence.
I press my pillow to my breast
As I caress the memory of your presence,
The sensitivity of your touch,
The intensity of your love.

Until morning,
Each breath I take
Absorbs the moments of passion,
And rekindles the fondling of
My deepest desires.
The gentle mist of your fragrance
Is reminiscent of the compassionate nature
Of your heart,
The depth of your soul.

Until morning,
I delight in the comfort
Of your subtle embrace.
No arms to hold me,
No words to inspire me,
And yet, I grasp hold of the weightlessness
Of your air....
Until morning.

S. Hafer Bronson

Don't Look in My Eyes

Thanks for a lovely evening.
Everything was divine.
I enjoyed your company.
I felt lost in time.

Now it's getting late.
I know you have to go.
But there's one more thing
I'd like for you to know.
This time spent with you
Has only confirmed,
A bittersweet lesson
That I've just learned.

I cannot pretend to be in control.
My feelings for you
Go beyond my soul.
I know you can tell.
I'm sure you realize,
That you've captured my heart
When you look in my eyes.

I know you don't need
To hear this from me.
But words go unspoken
Yet, I know you can see.
So, if it's too much
For you to surmise,
Let's just kiss,
Say goodnight,
But don't look in my eyes.

One Night in the Tropics

One night in the tropics
So steamy and hot.
Come join me, get ready.
Let's go to the spot
Where our minds lose focus,
Our reflexes give way,
To impulses, convulsions
That rock as we sway.

The breezes caress
As our bodies collide.
Submitting to desires
That can't be denied.
Your breath on my body
Compels me to probe,
From the family jewels
To your tender earlobes.

Don't leave me! Stay with me!
For we've just begun,
This night in the tropics
Neath the midnight sun.

S. Hafer Bronson

Let Me Put My Love on You

The eyes of love
Pierce the darkness of night.
The panting of desire.
Your tender kiss
Upon my lips
Begins to light my fire.

As hands move forward,
And members swell,
They develop minds of their own.
We anticipate the heavenly quake
As I holler and you moan.
Feelings give way to ecstasy
Our spirits take off in flight.
I hold you near and whisper in your ear,
"Oh Baby, you do me right!"

The joy of passion rises past
The moon, the stars, the sun!
You hold me near and whisper
"Dear, we've only just begun."

From this moment, My Sweet,
I will completely
Ravish you through and through.
I commit to your heart, say we'll never part,
Let me put my love on you.

Solitude

I ache for you.
I lay awake before I sleep…

Alone.

My thoughts drift to you
And your presence in my life.
I feel your tenderness.
I sense your desires.
I want nothing more
Than to satisfy your every need.

But you are not here with me,
So, I ache.

I ache to pull you close to me,
To touch your face, to kiss you,
To let my hands explore every
Crevasse of your body until…

But you are not here with me.
So, I ache.

Devotion

The tenderness found in a moment,
The touch of a loving hand.
The whispers of support and confidence,
All come from you, a Black man.

Who says that you are elusive,
Extinct, or hidden from view,
Or preferring vanilla to chocolate?
Oh no, my friend! Not you!

For you have felt the anguish
Of beauty beyond compare.
From the fullness of her tender lips
To the kinkiness of her hair.

As she surrenders to the fantasy
Of dreams that would not come true,
She finds the strength and care she needs
In the blackness and devotion
Of you!

Work Wid Da Brotha

I'll work with a brotha!
I ain't shame.
If you are in trouble,
Just call my name.
When darkness comes
And you can't see,
Just turn me on, Brotha,
I'll set you free.

I have watched you struggle
And will not deny,
That I'd sacrifice freedom
To have you by my side.
So smooth, so dark, so strong,
So pure.
So loving, so lonely and
So damned unsure.
I'll wipe your brow,
Your smile I'd shine.
Your back I'd rub,
Then blow your mind.

Don't you see, brotha?
You can depend on me,
To lift you higher
So you can see
Your worth, your strength,
Your future and your past.
I'll take the lead out of your tank
And take that foot out your ass.

I'm a real soul sista,
Tried and true.
But you have to want me
As much as I want you.
Work with a sista!
Call her name!
Cause success without compromise
Is a doggone shame.

Love the skin that you're in!
Sistas do! And that's a fact!
Be the man you were meant to be
Cause sistas got your back.

Intimacy

We are new to each other.
I understand that.
Yet, I find myself
Feeling the familiarity
That I crave.
Moving to the memory
Of your rhythm,
Shuddering at the thought of more.

As moistness overtakes me,
I forget how new we are.
All I can do is
React, respond and receive you
In a most comforting way.
Freely. Totally.
Intimately.

A Kiss Goodnight

Another day is ending.
Challenges flooded our day with thoughts
Of how to make it all better or
Better yet, how to make it all go away.
People, places and things ---
Some good, some not, either add to our challenges
or remind us what joy lies in simple things.
Simple things like a smile, a touch, a hug--
A kiss goodnight.

I want to come home to the simple things
That require only that I be there.
No qualifications or standards to meet,
Just me.
I am who I say I am.
I will be what God will have me to be.
And if you are with me, I will honor you the same--
With a long kiss goodnight.

Backdraft

I can't tell you how it happened
Or when it happened.
Somewhere between a smile
And a kiss,
Between now and then.
My fears are much like yours,
For the passion will fade.
The fantasies fulfilled
And then you'll go away.
You will have to.
You have commitments
That I will never be a part of.

I don't fool myself about that.
Yet, my emotions have
No effect on common sense.
I see you and my heart skips a beat.
You speak and my resistance diminishes.
I don't know what to do
Except to be fearful of my heart.

The sparks that fly each time we meet,
Have created a fire with a backdraft
That reduces me to ashes-
Ashes to be swept away
By your sensitivity and honesty,
Your kindness and your warmth.

S. Hafer Bronson

I don't feel right.
I'm not supposed to love you this way.
It is doomed and blameless.
It's not your fault,
Just my foolishness.

I'm afraid that I love you.
And I can't say it.

The Moment

If I had known you
Before or after this moment
Would we be the same?

Your words-- clear, sincere,
Your mind---sharp, focused.
Your life-- alone.

My words-- careful, detailed,
My mind-- a whirlwind of thoughts,
Orchestrated—Abandoned.

If I had loved you
Before or after this moment,
Would you have understood
That pain led me to discover the joy of you?

In this moment,
Challenged by love,
My heart searches to overcome the loneliness.
My soul surrenders
To Desire--the thread with which my soul will bind
In beauty and love
To share my life with yours.

S. Hafer Bronson

Insatiable Appetite

    Chocolatey
                Sweet
                              Delicious
                                              Treat
   Sticky
                Gooey
                              Sensational
                                              Chewy
  Melted
                Sticks
                              Tempting
                                              Licks
  Caramel
                Passion
                              Cowboy
                                              Fashion
  Lasting
                Pleasure
                              Beyond   Measure

First Impressions

Someone new has entered my life
And I am not afraid.
His physical presence seems masterful,
His words captivate my thoughts.
His eyes search for sincerity,
His heart bleeds my soul.

Someone new has entered my life.
I anticipate our next encounter.
My countenance cannot contain my joy.
My eyes mirror my thoughts.
My thoughts propel my soul
To touch his life
As he has touched mine.

S. Hafer Bronson

You Warm My Heart

You have a gift for love.
Your essence draws and binds
Your compassion to others
Who would only share a moment
And forget things worthwhile.

You have a love for life
That can see tomorrow
And transcend regrets
Of yesterday.

You have a life of promises
That although cultivated with pride,
Will at times fall seeds
That cannot thrive.

The beauty of love is that
It touches without feeling.
The beauty of caring is that
It spreads freely.
The beauty of togetherness
Is found in oneness,
Unconditional oneness
That survives a need
To sometimes be alone.

You warm my heart
Because you understand.

Visions

Let me enjoy
Your voice, your smile.
You can go home tomorrow.
Don't leave
And rob me of this precious time.
Please, don't add to my sorrow.

Let me pretend
That you are mine
This morning, noon and night.
Relax, forget, unwind, be mine
And let imagination take flight.

Your face, your lips your eyes, your being
Are my source of contentment and joy.
I need you now
To inspire my heart.
Don't walk out the door.

Visions of us in a timeless place
Where love and caressing abound.
No worries, no fears,
Only us, my dear,
With no one else around.

Come, dance and feel
The joy in my heart,
Ecstatic impulses to and fro.
Let's love and laugh and love some more.
You can go home tomorrow.

Empowerment

The personification of self-awareness through knowledge and encouragement.

When the Black Lady Sings: Musings of an African American Princess

Greatness

I wake up in the morning
And while getting out of bed,
I immediately envision a crown upon my head.
A day of living in front of me,
Misery buried during sleep.
My joy found in the morning
Where HE told me it would be.

As I regally walk across the room
To ready myself for the day,
I waste no time or brain cells
On what other folks will say.

You see, I was born to greatness
And in order to achieve,
I must embrace my blackness
For it is all in me.

The soul of my existence,
Established long before my reign.
The strength of my heritage pulsing
Like African drumbeats in my veins.

Each footstep measured by wisdom and strength
My gait laced with faith and hope.
My confidence laced with knowledge
My vision, with endless scope.

I embody the color of change.
There is very little that I lack.
For my soul is nurtured by the omnipotence of God,
And the greatness of being Black.

Storm

Our journey of life would be meaningless without challenges.
Sometimes the battle is easy and we walk away unscathed.
At other times we struggle with the thought of another day,
Living with the agony that life has put in our path.

Be still.

Embrace the spark that ignites your soul
And lights your path to Forgiveness.
Let it catch fire with a force that no storm can extinguish.
You are a blessing to those of us who witness your struggle.
There is a strength in you that will carry all of us through.

Storms will batter and bruise us,
Weathering Hope.
But hopelessness recedes when artistry is revealed,
Through the beauty of a soul guided by Love.

Be still and KNOW
You are beautiful.
You are loved.
And you are never alone.

S. Hafer Bronson

What Good Can Come of It?

Would you come and stay the night?
Could I define your presence in my life?
Would our longing stand the test of time?
Could I be yours and you be mine?

I don't pretend to understand
What makes you such a driven man.
I only know that emotionally
My heart is full of uncertainty.
I see, I want, I need, I feel.
But fear to speak affects my will.

What good can come of love this time?
When what we are has not been defined?

Combination

You
Loved me once,
You
Loved me twice
But you won't love me again.
The speed at which you satisfy,
Has worn my patience thin.
The love you say
You have for me
Must cease being explored.
The ragdoll effect
You have on my back
Is a malady I can't afford.

You
Do not answer when I call or
You say you're on the other line.
Yet,
When your need for love surmounts,
You
Quickly star sixty-nine.

I like you.
That goes without saying.
But believe me
I love myself more.
And while I acknowledge
Your "loving" attempts,
I can't see you anymore.

S. Hafer Bronson

Don't Underestimate Me

I am resilient.
I bounce.
I hurt.
I heal.
I'm forceful, though shy.
My eyes reflect my soul's weaknesses.
My countenance reflects my strengths.
I fall, but rise to complete
What I've begun.

Love solo does not fulfill.
Rejection dims the light in my soul.
Yet, in time, I'll love again.
Don't underestimate me.
I know fulfillment comes from within.
My heart and mind
Will carry the impact of my sorrow.
But I know His grace will sustain.

Pride

Oh God! Please help me!
I don't understand.
He was unarmed.
Gunned down.
Not quite yet a man.
You killed him for jaywalking?
You blew him away?
The cameras were watching.
It didn't happen like you said.

His hands in the air,
Don't shoot!
I heard him cry.
You shot him like a rabid dog
And then we watched him die.

Wasn't it bad enough
That you sent their grandfathers to war?
If they weren't blown to bits,
They came back full of Agent Orange.
No cameras to warn us,
No reporters who knew
The real devastation of that witches' brew.

And let's not forget
That Desert Storm.
Destroying the promises
Of lives unborn.

S. Hafer Bronson

Their fathers and mothers
Plucked by the bush.
Baked in the desert
Then hid the abuse.

Mothers without fathers,
Fathers without sons,
Children without parents,
Everyone carrying guns.

Now another one is lying
Dead in the street.
Wearing a hoodie,
A box of skittles and a cell phone
At his feet.

I'm beginning to wonder
If we ever mattered at all.
The younger they are,
The faster they fall.

When did we enter into this war?
What the hell are we fighting for?

I love America.
God knows I do.
But in this moment,
I'm not proud of you.

Abstract

Those eyes...
You hide your soul in brightness, yet in plain sight.
I look for a slither of your pulse within the view.
It is not there.

Those lips...
Arched so full and graceful,
Awaiting a long, forgiving kiss—
An encore to the pleasure that once lived there forever.

Your hair...
The sprinkling of wisdom introduced
Through love and pain,
And more love, and more pain.

And innocence...
Innocence that declares the truth yet finds deceit.
Innocence that reaches to embrace true love yet,
Becomes entrapped in indecisive games.

Do not hide your shoulders, broad and wide,
They are your strength.
They will endure the weight of your journey.
Know that every journey has an end.
Within every sleeper is a dream.
Rest well.

S. Hafer Bronson

The Betrayal

I am hurt.
I am hurt because I chose to trust
In a desire to belong with someone.
I willingly exposed my dreams
To a stranger.
One who caressed my thoughts
And eased my pain.
But the pain eased is nothing
Compared to the hurt I feel.

I GIVE UP!
I CAN'T DO THIS ANYMORE!

I see no purpose for this pain,
No strength in its resolve.
Emotions run fast and hot.
And like all fires that burn hot,
All that remains are spent embers,
Not yet cold but smothered
By the waste of a heated
ONE NIGHT STAND!

Widow's Peak

He walked into the room
And saw her
Sitting near the door.

He tagged his friends
And asked, "Hey, Yall,
Have you seen her here before?"

Her fine brown frame
Put others to shame.
Her hair coiffed into place.
Her eyes like pools.
I must stay cool.
Can't let her
See me sweat.

He watched her rise
And cross the floor.
Her steps as light as air,
Drew men like flies
To his surprise.
She pretended not to care.

His buddies turned
And looked away.
None of them would speak.
They turned their backs
And whispered "Man,
Beware of Widow's peak."

S. Hafer Bronson

She came at him with lips ablaze,
Assessed him from head to toe.
She took his hand
And scratched his palm.
Then said, "Come on, let's go."

He left the stool,
Oh what a fool!
Reacting to desire.
Across the floor and out the door,
His loins were set on fire.

As passion locked the hotel door,
And clothes began to fall,
The hours passed
And they collapsed,
Not moving anymore.

He turned to kiss her
One more time
But something was not right.
He felt a pain move up his arm,
His chest was feeling tight.

He started panting
Hard and fast.
She thought he wanted more.
But when she reached
To give him joy,
He rolled
And hit the floor.

Call 911, he tried to say,
As sweat poured
From his face.
She looked amused,
Not at all confused
By what had taken place.

"You lasted
Longer than most,"
She said.
"I'll have to give you that.
You made me purr and arch my back,
Just like a kitty cat."

"You see,
My name is Widow.
I'm insatiable, you see.
My thirst for love
Continues on
Until I reach my peak.

I thank you for your service,"
She stated with a grin.
"And if I thought
You could handle it,
I'd sex you once again."

My heartbeat
Continued to quicken.
My eyes were seeing double.
And as I listened to her words,
I knew I was in trouble.

I knew I had to stay calm. Breathe.
Don't panic. Close your eyes.
I slowly regained my composure,
Pushed anxiety aside.

And then I heard the door shut.
I listened. I was alone.
Thank God, I said.
But how
Will I get my black ass
Back home?

It serves me right for thinking
That I was the super freak.
I was a fool
And I got schooled
In the web of Widow's peak.

Everything's Cool

My life is in order.
I'm in control.
I can call your bluff
Or play any role.
My hunger for life
Will never wane.
Once I'm satisfied,
I start over again.

Don't expect me to be
Like your neighbors or friends.
My style is my own.
I never pretend.

I've traveled to faraway places and yet,
Not easily impressed by the people I've met.

My passions run deep
As I work towards a goal.
There's no doubt in my mind
That I'm in control.

Drama

I heard
Him say
She told
Her that
You saw
Me do that.

Let me
Tell you
They don't know
Just who
They're messing with.

All this
He said
She said
I said
We were
All but through.
Baby tell me
Who's my lover?
He, she, it or you?

I can't deal with
All this mess,
Loose tongues
And empty minds.

If they
Had a
Life worth living
They wouldn't be
Messing in mine.

You believe
Whatever you like.
Three strikes,
You're out with me.
So I will
Leave you
With the
Drama.
Cause that's where you wanna be.

S. Hafer Bronson

Gray

You have a voice that claims authority
Over each word you speak.
Sought out by many,
Endeared to only a few.
Your choice.

Your hair boldly proclaims
Years of life proudly spent,
Noticeably full and reminiscent of
Life your way.

Your body maps your experiences,
Various artistic signatures, different strokes.
Marks of innocence, scars of persecution,
Badges of determination and courage.

Gray enhances the wisdom
Of your years.
It proclaims the right to seek
Whatever you wish life to be.
There is no need to shout.
Gray speaks softly but with a reverberation
That allows your peace to be heard.
Calmly, boldly and forevermore
Gray.

Forecast: Rain

I look out the window,
And I see clouds forming-
Thick puffy clouds,
Growing darker as
They move slowly across the sky.

And in their wake,
A fine mist sprays the atmosphere.
Progressing into a light cleansing
Of the earth's surface.

In a moment,
The hard rain will come
To eliminate the dryness,
To bring hope back into barren soil.

The heavy downpour
Floods the soaked land.
The water stands, for
It has no place to go.
(Too much too fast.)
As the storm passes,
The earth waits to accept the gift.
That will help to renew
The promise of forgiveness.

S. Hafer Bronson

Inner Visions

You're in my mind.
You've pierced my heart
And breathed life back
Into my soul.

A mundane existence
Creating contentment within
Expected views.
I won't complain.
I made it so.
Now as I break away
To find the serenity
Of a spirit in flight,
I carry with me
The knowledge of self
And accomplished grace.

I bow to my past,
While in the present,
Contemplating constant mercy.
A future unwritten,
Fearing less and
Reaching beyond the finite
Into endless dreams.

When the Black Lady Sings: Musings of an African American Princess

S. Hafer Bronson

Passages

All of life's passages can lead to healing.

S. Hafer Bronson

Journey

I'm not scared to let you know
That I am afraid
Of Newness-----
The unexpected opportunity to
Explore unknown regions
Of hot deserts, deep waters,
Rocky terrain, cool plains.

I'm not afraid to let you know
That I'm scared
Of Familiarity-----
The complacent accumulation
Of sameness,
Too much, yet not enough
Routine, not satisfying,
Necessary comfort.

But right now
I need passion.
I need tenderness.
I need consistency.
I need for us to bring delight
To this Moment,
This unexpected opportunity,
To enjoy the Newness,
Anticipate the Familiarity,
And to Rediscover
Suppressed Desires.

The Touch

We walked to the theatre
To see a picture show.
I don't remember my exact age.
It was so long ago.
A nice sunny day, no clouds in the sky.
As we stepped with excitement,
My brothers and I.

As we entered the movies and took our seats,
All I could think of was getting something to eat.
The coins that I carried burned a hold in my hand,
As I dreamed of sodas and candy
At the concession stand.

So I arose from my seat to make my snack choice,
But when I reached the top of the aisle
I heard an older voice.
"Come here little girl.
I have something for you to see.
I only let special people accompany me.
I am the reel man. I run the show.
If it weren't for me, the movies won't go.
Don't you want to come with me and see how I do it?
It will just take a moment and you'll never forget it."

"No thank you, I'd better not.
The movie is about to begin.
My brothers are waiting,
And I have to hurry to get back in."

"Remember," He said. "I control the movies and lights.
Your brothers won't know the difference. It'll be alright.
I'll even give you a quarter and I'll do nothing wrong.
You can use the money to get a foot-long."

He reached into his pocket and extended his hand.
Then I entered the world of the movie reel man.

There was something odd about him,
Although young, I could see
His features and countenance
Were very different from me.
He swayed as he walked,
His balance not sure.
I realized my mistake in accepting the lure.

Reaching the top,
I turned back to find
The reel man behind me
So, I spoke my mind.

"I don't want to be here,
I want to go back.
My brothers are waiting
To get their snacks."

As I moved to find the stairs,
He blocked my way.
His eyes now were glassed over
In a growing rage.
He took my arm
And stood in front of me.
"But you haven't seen yet
What I brought you to see."
He turned me around,
And quickly showed me the reel.

His hands found my waist
And he started to feel.
He held me with one hand
And felt me with another.
All I could think of was
Where are my brothers?
I told the man NO
But he was so strong.
I was only six or seven
But I knew this was wrong.

I told him my brothers were waiting for me
And then in that moment, he set me free.
I ran down the stairs,
Forgetting the treats.
I was so full of fear,
I wanted nothing to eat.
I returned to my brothers
In the theater row.
I was not even certain if I should let them know.
So I sat through the movies
And when it was time to go,
We all left together and talked about the show.

Half way back to grandma's
I decided to tell
About what happened to me
And the man with the reel.

It went in one ear and then out the other,
(So much for protection from my two big brothers).
The blame was all mine,
So I dared not repeat
What happened that day
When I went for my treat.
As years passed by,

S. Hafer Bronson

I would never forget
How the movie reel man
Tried to make me his pet.

I never could name him,
Yet his face is still clear.
And when I see him now,
I still shake with fear.

He doesn't remember me,
Those kind never do.
Real men don't do that,
But reel men do.

New Beginnings

A fleeting moment,
A sudden glance.
A name, a number,
To find romance.

A mind, a heart,
A soul to heal.
A chance to remember
How love feels.

S. Hafer Bronson

In Remembrance Of....

Sometimes, there is pain-
Unspeakable pain that weakens my heart.
Sometimes there is fear-
A paralyzing uneasiness that
Keeps me from moving forward.

At times, the sadness
Seems to flow without tears,
And the anger steadily creates
An insurmountable wall of despair.
At times, the emptiness
Invades my solitude and
Ravages my strength.
All of these things happen
Because you are no longer here.

It cannot end this way.
I can't give grief permission
To dismantle the intent of your love.
Somewhere, amid my sorrow,
I know that
There is a faith and courage
That leaves little room for fear.
Within me, there is a strong will
That can make unordinary pain release its grip.

Your lessons of perseverance are not lost.
My life does continue.
It's just that sometimes,
There is pain.

Epic

You were an African king.
i served you.
You ruled a nation.
i submitted to your desires.

THEN

You were captured.
Shackled by inequity, greed and power.
i followed to serve a master
Not of my choosing.
Foreign tongues, bestial ways,
Violation, pain, misery.
i sought you to bond, to sustain
To remember, to dream...

OF BEING FREE

Chains of color and anger
Mark your steps.
You cannot be a man.
Tongues once foreign
Refuse to cease.
Degradation, hate, greed, fear.
Violation, pain, misery.
i watched as you
Found solace in the brotherhood
Of wine and song.

i listened as you spoke
Of dreams not realized,
A people divided.
i grew tired of the loneliness,
Violation, misery and pain.
i watched, i listened, i learned.
I grew stronger,
Determined to rule in my African kingdom
Until my king returns to his place of nobility.
Your dreams became my thoughts,
My plan to honor and respect your greatness,
But I can no longer serve you.

FOR NOW,

I must be free
To toil, to plant to cultivate the seeds
Of a dying nation
With faith, honor and a determination

TO SURVIVE.

An Understanding

I want love to nurture my life.
To feed that which hungers within me.
To caress that which has already been fulfilled.
To understand my insecurities,
And to provide me with the strength
To stand strong in my convictions.

For me, loving is
More emotional than spiritual,
More intimate than sexual.
A sympathetic ear, a touch
That can be felt by my heart.
A caring glance or simultaneous
Thoughts of each other.

I do not want to be afraid of love.
When love is founded in trust,
There is no need to fear
That love won't last.

Love accepts the imperfections of humanity-
The errors and mistakes of a lifetime.
It does not condemn. It soothes.
It does not reject. It compromises
Without robbing one's identity.
I am who I am because of love.
Therefore, I must accept myself
Before I can freely love anyone else.

S. Hafer Bronson

Paces

I've grown old enough
To understand that life
Can be frustrating.

Much of life is spent
Confronting obligations that
Subdue our passion.
Frustrating because
True passion can't be put aside.

Anxiety surpasses each
Second by a minute.
Time is lost.
Feelings sink.
Be careful!
Passion may wane!

I don't want to lose it.
I don't want my passion
To fall behind.

Pace it!

Give it time.
Study patience and
Keep frustration at bay.
There must be a way to...

Pace it!

Walk with a gait

That is steady.
In which a misstep
Is not an indication of failure,
But a source of strength
That binds my passion to my goal.

Pace it!

Until aggression
Lengthens my stride,
Creating a widening gap,
Between my fears and my love.
My passion.

Closed Doors

He Said:
> I love you.
> You know that.
> But I'm no good for you.
> We've become such good friends
> And I want to be fair to you.
> You're a beautiful person,
> Inside and out.
> You're the one for me,
> Without a doubt.
> But I am a loner.
> My life is a mess.
> And I don't want to keep you
> From happiness.
> You've accomplished a lot
> In your life on your own.
> The best thing for me to do
> Is to leave you alone.

She Said:
> Yes, we are friends,
> And I love you, too.
> I know that I am not the one for you,
> I'm just not your type.
> I've said it before.
> So why does it hurt to close this door?

He Said:
>
> The times that we've talked of
> Our lives and our dreams
>
> Have stirred mixed emotions
> That led to extremes.
> I've shared things with you
> That were hard to admit.
> Your eyes see right through me.
> They know my intent.
> So why is it that I can't let you go?
>
> Why does my need for you
> Continue to grow?
> I can't name your place in my life, it's true.
> You've been my confidante, a friend I can trust.
> But you deserve love from me,
> Not just moments of lust.

She Said:
>
> I know that you've struggled
> With what we should be.
> I've learned to be patient,
> I know you've needed me.
> You're strong and independent
> But your direction, unclear.
> I only wanted to calm your fears.
>
> I can't accept loving you
> When it's traded for flesh.
> It only brings misery, not happiness.
> So let's walk away.
> Don't say anything more.
> While we can leave
> Just by closing, not slamming, the door.

S. Hafer Bronson

Endings

I thanked the Lord above
When I discovered your love.
Your lips, your touch, your taste,
Sent me into outer space.
But when I came back down,
You were nowhere to be found.

Silence was all I could hear,
From one I held so dear.
I did not understand
What had become of our plan.
I waited, patiently, steadfast,
Until too much time had passed.
I realized the nature of the game.
Now I just feel ashamed.

I thought your mind was clear.
I thought your words, sincere.
I thought you loved me true.
As I indeed loved you.

But time surely knows the way,
To expose those who just want to play.
Another lesson, another hurt, another sigh.
But the hardest?
Another unsaid goodbye.

Farewell

You called to say you loved me,
You said I'd see you soon.
But now I feel abandoned
Like the sky without the moon.

I waited 'til it hurt so much,
I couldn't bear to even think your name.
It took me a while to realize
That things were not the same.

After nights of contemplation,
After days of wondering why.
Reality resumed its place,
And I no longer cry.

I realize my strength
Did not begin or end with you.
It comes from He Who Has No Name,
For He always sees me through.

Farewell my love,
Don't worry.
No need to feel ashamed.
I never let silent frustration
Keep me from calling His name.

The sun can be hidden by storm clouds.
The moon cut in half in the sky.
Yet, they always resume their glory.
And so, my dear, will I.

S. Hafer Bronson

In the Mourning

A precious life has moved from earth to eternity.
Tears weaken logic
As the reality of loss creeps into our lives.
Hearts ache from the separation of physical from the spirit.

Mourning comes.

As the mourning comes, we reflect on a life well lived,
Of smiles and moments that endear us to the laughter in her spirit.

She is free.

Yet, her freedom comes at a cost to those of us who must linger.
We will hold on to the years of memories
And love and unconditional acceptance.

We will mourn her release from the physical but with vision,
Find and continue to carry the spark which ignited her spirit.

Pay it forward.

Love life and each other.
Embrace, comfort and remember.
Find laughter beyond the tears,
So that we may all find
Joy in the mourning.

Honor

Regardless of what is going on around you,
It is never out of place to honor your own spirit.
Honor and feed your strength because
It has brought you a long way.

Honor the sacrifices of others,
For they laid the groundwork for your successes.
Honor the bonds you share with your children
For they are your connection to immortality
And proof that there is still good in the world.

Recognize the love that still pours from your heart
For those who hurt all around.
Your love is plentiful,
Your journey, long and I pray unfinished.

Whether you are alone or with many,
Thank someone, anyone, everyone
For raising you.
And know that you will never truly be alone.

S. Hafer Bronson

Did You Love Me, Ever?

It is over.
Any opportunity that I could have had to know you is gone.
Sitting here, blocking out the words of faith and encouragement.
Sitting next to siblings I never knew.
Wondering if they really knew you either.
Travelling Man. That is what they called you.
Can I get an "Amen"?

I don't even know what to call you.
Father? Daddy? Dad?
When was the last time you saw me?
Was it also the first time?
You were never hidden from me.
I just could never find you.
Did you even remember me?
Did you know my name?
Did you love me, ever?

Mom's memories of you faded long ago.
Never a smile when your name was mentioned.
Never a harsh word.
I guess that comes with accepting responsibility
For your actions.
Were you as kind to her memory as she was to yours?
Did you love her, ever?

Well, Travelling Man, the journey has ended.
Time to let go.
Just to let you know, I am doing just fine.
Oh yeah! Just as soon as the court removes this ankle bracelet
I will be just fine!

I joined a gang instead of enjoying a pickup game with you.
I enjoyed crack rather than an evening of cowboy movies on the couch with you.
I went to prison and renamed a convict instead of college to become an educated man.
I knew better. I just couldn't do better.

Mom was strong but
She wasn't strong enough to be a man.
I needed you for that.
I needed for you to
Show me some love.

I can't hate you.
I can't love you.
And I will never know
If you loved me, ever.

S. Hafer Bronson

Merging Lives

My heart feels the burden of your life.
Oldest son, educated one.

Obligations weigh so heavily.
They collapse self-fulfilling dreams.
You can't afford self-pity.
There is too much to do.

Fear of failure compels you to success.
But, seemingly, pride in success is
Unfulfilling.
Whose success is it, anyway?

By nature of birth, you are.
By strength of character, you become.
For obligation, you perform.
For love, you make sacrifices.

How can you be everything to all
And no one to yourself?

How is it that we learn
To find strength in adversity?
When did we come to understand that
Focus is paramount to success?

The struggle between "need" and "must"
Is debilitating, and yet, with each choice,
A new strength emerges and in a strange way,
A burden is lifted.

My desire for you is that the circle of life,
As it comes around, will supply your needs,
And continue to strengthen you
As you do what you must do.

S. Hafer Bronson

Final Notice

We've had a magnificent journey together.
I wouldn't change a thing about it.
We've smiled and laughed
And shared sorrows. Deep sorrows.

Distant lovers
Friends undercover
Sharing intimacies that
Most only dream about.

Time has now become our enemy.
We both made choices.
Our decision based on love and dignity.
Our own.
Before you go
I ask that you do one more thing.
Call me.

I don't want to be caught off guard.
I don't want my primal screams
To be heard by a stranger.
I don't want you to believe for
One moment that you will not be missed.
I don't want you to think for one minute
That I didn't love you.
So please,
Call me before you go.

Your walk through life was quiet
But not remarkably uneventful.
You created legacies with passion
Establishing your independence
During a time when the struggle
Was still in its infancy.
You achieved. You explored.
You cared. You loved. You lived.
Now you feel it is time for you to die.

Oddly enough, I understand.
We both know that the decision
Was made without conflict or struggle.
I know you are at peace.

You are a jewel.
I've always known it,
Though I would ignore
What was really happening
Between us.
A lasting, mutual friendship where
Our last shared time together
Will always be our best.
So please,
Call me before you go.

We have never denied each other intimacy.
I would feel cheated
If you left without allowing me
One more moment of tenderness.
Allow me one more chance
At rebirth.
So beautiful and pure.
Before you die.

Identity

That which makes us who we are.

Proof of existence.

S. Hafer Bronson

Tyrone

I know it hurts,
But it's not what you think.
Come sit down beside me,
Let's have a drink.

We're grown, we're adults,
We can handle this.
Don't throw us away
Over one little kiss!

Okay, so I held her
A little too close.
But she got her hair caught
In her earring post.
I was trying to free her....
Wait! Wait!
Baby please!
As GOD as my witness
On bended knees!

I was only trying to help
A female in distress,
When you saw me give money
To her for that dress.
She didn't have enough money,
It was only a loan,
'Til she stopped by the ATM
On her way home.

What do you mean
"Can it get any worse?"
She forgot her credit cards
When she changed her purse!

AIN'T NO makeup on my collar!
AIN'T NO perfume on my clothes!

You know that I love YOU!
And only God knows,
How those panties got under
The seat of my Benz.
Who told you that?
Damn!
Here we go again!

I DON'T KNOW THAT WOMAN!

I got you!
You so fine!
Don't believe what you hear
On the Nigger News line.

Calm down, sit down baby.
Let me say what I feel.
We both know that our love is real!

My heart is so full,
My words can't express,
How you've brought me such joy
And happiness.

Oh baby,
You know how I get when you cry.
You know me too well for me to lie.
Let's go up to bed and talk some more.
Just give me a minute to lock the door.

Go on upstairs
While I get this phone.
"Hello?
What's up baby?
Yeah. I'm here alone."

Angelina

In all my life,
Not in my wildest dreams,
Could I have imagined
Such trying things.
My years as a daughter,
Were marred with neglect.
My years as a lover
I haven't gotten right yet.
My years as a mother
Filled with joy and pain.
The loss of my children
Will forever remain.

And yet, in my life,
 I have always known,
The Lord as my Savior, Companion,
And so.....
I think of my blessings,
The strength I received,
From surviving these battles
Because
I BELIEVE!

Billy

You come to me at night
During restless sleep.
Your broad shoulders beckon me
To seek comfort there.
Your eyes listen intensely
To my fears
And soothe my racing heart.
I am not alone.

I look to you,
But you never speak.
You reach for my hand.
Your touch brings back memories
That make me feel your love once more.
I am protected by your spirit.
For this I will always be grateful.
God has chosen that death
Not break this bond between us.
He understands better than I ever will.
Secrets that we kept inside
Are only made known
By His grace and our love.
You've always been my comfort,
Now and forever.

Identity

I wish that I could say that your name was my gift to you.
The truth is that your parents gave you this gift.
Your name is such an important part of your life.
It is who you are.

As a child your parents loved you and guided
Your steps in life, because they understood
Your strengths and weaknesses.
And when you allow them to,
The memory of their lessons
Can counsel you
In the realization of your dreams.

When I heard your name, after meeting you,
I wondered, 'how could this be?'
Did every man with this name possess
The same qualities?
I think so.

The differences occur because of how those qualities are developed.

Some are buried by errors of judgment as life progresses.

Your parents must have been fine human beings.
For no other reason, I thank them for the gift of you.
They love you as you are,
And so do I.

Ricki Lake

I am nothing.
I live my life, I touch, I share.
I care about men who can't love
Anyone but themselves.
No matter how big the space,
Their egos fill the room.
There is no room for me here.
No place for my feelings to be sensed,
No receiver to hear my thoughts.
It belongs to them alone.
I wish them well.
I must go on.

I'm convinced that my purpose in living
Is greater, of more significance,
Than satisfying the egomaniacal ravings
Of middle aged assholes whose credo in life
Is "Feed Me."
Damn it, I have a heart, I have a soul.

I have feelings!

I want more than you can spare to give.
So guess what?

I'm gone!

The Preacher

If I could be effective
In everything I do,
Turn mountains into molehills,
Change other's point of view.
Let everything begin with me,
With immeasurable wealth, times two.
Then Lord, I'd be successful,
And I'd do it all for you.

Seek and ye shall find, my child
Ask and it shall be given.
But you cannot serve two masters,
One here and one in heaven.
Love, when shared, can conquer all
And lead you to success.
But don't assume that monetary wealth
Will bring peace and happiness.
You have the power to lead a life
That's blessed from heaven above.
But the greatest gift I can give to you
Is the power and strength of my love.

The Teacher

You are my teacher.
I do not expect miracles from the lessons you teach,
Only understanding.
I don't assume that you know all,
Because you don't.

I want to know what you have learned about:

Life
      Love
            Hurt
                   Religion
                          People
                                   Cruelty.

But I want to teach you about:

Life
      Love
            Hate
                   Anger
                          Forgiveness.

Forgiveness does not mean that you are foolish.
It simply means that you realize that hatred
Destroys men's hearts and clouds judgment.
It benefits no one. It kills desire, passion, faith and love.
It leaves you stranded and trapped in a way of thinking
That will ruin any chance for happiness because you
Won't be able to see it.

Teacher, your heart and mind hold so much pain and anger.
Why are you so angry with yourself?
Those who caused you pain have been removed from you.
Why do you anguish?
Why do you blame yourself for the cruelty of another?
Why do you let them win?

You are good but do not see God there.
You are kind, but do not realize that it comes to you
Through God's love.
You are His child and my friend.

My teacher.

S. Hafer Bronson

Sweet

The feeling began long before I knew you.
It started in a place where emotions had no real boundaries
And there was no meaning attached to what life was all about.

It began in the arms of my grandmother,
Whom I think knew me and loved
Me more than anyone on this earth.
Although our time together was brief, she is a part of my soul.

Sweet.

A sensation of total, nonjudgmental acceptance
Still comforts me when I think of her.

Sweet.

My eyes did not challenge her.
My shyness did not discourage her.
She loved me and I do believe
That she saw bits of herself in me.

Oh, how she would hold me and mash me against her bosom!
Each time I recall this memory, I feel her heart close to me,
Her love so near and protecting.
So missed.

Sweet.

I have held her name close to my bosom
Until now.
You have taken me back to that place where
Emotions should have no boundaries.

I needed to find some way to honor
The memories of what I felt with her,
And what I feel with you.
No other word can describe it like.....

Sweet.

S. Hafer Bronson

Black Snake

You say there is nothing to fear.
It is good.
You say that the benefits
Far outweigh my fears.
I don't know about that.

A black snake
Has nothing to do
But be a snake.
I try convincing myself
That it's his nature
To seek a warm place.

Snakes are cold-blooded.
When it finds that place,
It coils and basks itself
In the heat.
Size doesn't matter.
All black snakes want the same thing.

Instinctively when I see
A black snake, I coil, too.
I've read in books about
Its harmless nature.

Yet, I don't believe.
I have seen how quickly
It slithers away.
So graceful.

I was mesmerized by the
Sleekness and preciseness
Of its tongue and the dexterity of its jaws.
Fascinating.
Fulfilling.
Striking.
So cold.
Black snake.

S. Hafer Bronson

Sonny Clark's Blues

A good morning sometimes turns into a bad day.
Being a good man doesn't seem to change that.
The burdens of life, the aches of unfulfilled dreams,
The frustration of my inability to find
Resolution and peace.
My blues are all mine but too heavy to bear alone.

Then I come home to you.
Your arms outstretched to remove
The heavy burden from my shoulders.
Your voice eases the tension and worry of my mind.
Your silence affirms my choices.
Your soft shoulders become a place for my head to fit
When my thoughts pound away at my strength and my will.

You bring rejuvenation and renewed focus to my life.
You fortify me; you understand my nature, my soul.
As long as I breathe, I will need you.
As long as I feel, I will love you.
As long as I ache, I pray that you will be there
To feed my hungry soul.

Miss Helen

I think about a lot of things.
But you've never seen me pray.
I have lived longer than I expected.
I guess that is a good thing.
I have made it through some hard times.

You know, I lost two daughters.
My oldest left this world many years ago,
Taken from me in a fit of rage.
She was my oldest child.
My other daughter, though lost,
Is still among us.
She just fell into the crack in the floor.

The pain does terrible things to me sometimes.
I sit and think about it but you've never seen me pray.
Comfort is hard to find but easy to fix.

Family.
I just want my family whole and happy.
Parenting didn't come with instructions.
Maybe my examples were not good enough.

Still,
I wait by the phone or listen for the doorbell to ring.
At this point in my life all I want is time with my family.
Maybe one day soon one of them will come by,
Sit a while and chat with me
And the little girl who sits in the chair by the door.

S. Hafer Bronson

Nirka's Kitchen

Welcome to my humble home.
It has been many years since we have seen each other
But the sight of you warms me still.
Cuba libre!

Come into my kitchen,
Where I have prepared for you
The best I have to offer.
Please sit. Let us talk of life and memories.

My kitchen and I have aged well.
It serves me and I serve from it.
It breaks down, I break down.
Fifty years of fixes have not harmed either of us.
I am a very resourceful woman!

Would you like a glass of water?
My refrigerator cools,
Not as well as it used to.
So, ice is a specialty reserved for drinks.

My refrigerator is older than I
But a little duct tape on both of us,
And we hum right along!

Yes, my life is simple but
I prefer it this way.
My neighbors are my friends,
We depend on each other's kindness.
Sharing, it is not such a bad thing.

I hope you will enjoy the meal.
It is not much but it is all I have.
We are friends, always. You understand.
Cuba Libre!

The Art of Seduction

We are entering into moments together
That require no words.
Body parts respond with just a thought.
Shuttering images of two becoming one.
Sensual visualizations of fusing minds,
Locked in an ever mounting search for ecstasy
In each other's arms.
It does not end where it begins.
I must touch you. I must taste you.
I must validate that my senses are not simply responding
To the physical.
I want to truly understand that
You.....are.....real.

I want to find and reclaim
The part of what I see of me, in you.
I know of no other way than to
Search your being with my heart and soul.
And in doing so I will give up to you
Those things of yours that I have claimed
As my own.
Sensuality, tenderness, patience
And a hint of innocence.

So it seems,
That I am ready to move from the
Art of seduction
To.....
The seduction of Art.

Walt

Smile.
Therein lies the peace in your soul.
It shines through the tiny hints of joy
That curves your lips and
Causes your pupils to gleam with contentment.

There is a vision of serenity that
Claims priority over your will.
Calm. Caring.
Cautiously feeling
What is, what could be.

Required loneliness is
A necessary infusion for your spirit
To connect with the peace in your soul.

Live well. Dream well. Be fulfilled.
It is well within your reach,
For He has made it so.

S. Hafer Bronson

A Nun's Tale

Give me a Sista
With a long black dress.
All covered up
Wearing a cross on her chest.

Give me a Sista with locks
Hidden from view.
No matter where she was,
She had her eyes on you.

A rosary at her waist.
Black shoes on her feet.
With a pep in her step
And a yearning to teach.

Face framed in white,
A love of God to uphold.
Shaping young minds
To go for the gold.

When she walked in a room,
We stood out of respect.
Girls curtseyed, boys bowed,
Wow! The things you don't forget!

All noise would cease,
All heads to the front.
We prayed before class,
Before AND after lunch.

As she floated through the day
On the wings of her Faith,
She taught us not to tarry
For time does not wait.

Be kind to each other.
But if you lost control,
Punishment was swift
For she had other minds to mold.

Yes, give me a Sista
From O.S.P.*
Thank God for His blessings
Given through her.... to me!

*Oblate Sisters of Providence

S. Hafer Bronson

Warmest Regards

It's time once again
To recognize you
As a good friend
Even though our friendship is new.
.

We've know each other
For such a short while.
And it's further complicated
By the distance in miles.
Yet, whenever we talk,
Wherever we meet,
Your presence still warms me,
Your voice, just as sweet.

Your kindness, your thoughtfulness
Only increase.
As you live and grow,
To be what you can be.

As you challenge the old
To discover the new,
Here's a toast!
Happy Birthday
To the Newness
Of you!

Sister

When your journey seems difficult
And hard to understand,
Just put your faith
In the Father's hands.
Let go and let God
Be your Master and Guide.
His promises can clear your thoughts
And wipe the tears from your eyes.

Be patient with yourself,
We are all here to grow.
Make past mistakes memories,
Then just let go.

Things happen with reason,
Sometimes unknown to man.
I can't ease your troubled heart.
But believe me,
God can!

S. Hafer Bronson

Cousin, Mine

I didn't know you,
But I did care.
I searched for family
And found you there.
My grandma's brother,
He was the sire.
His parents loved you
But he aimed higher.

Your other grandma,
She loved you, too.
You moved away.
I never knew.
Decades would pass
Without a word.
But life has cycles
That cleanse and purge.

The way was cleared
For us to meet.
And once we did,
I felt complete.
Your eyes, your smile,
The same as mine
Your life, your spirit,
So well defined.

I see in you
Joy and relief.
I felt in my heart
A sense of grief.
We had to lose
In order to gain.
The heritage we sought
Found in our name.

S. Hafer Bronson

Panther

I was....

Struggle was the buzzword.
Freedom from oppression our goal.
Unity of purpose with defined organization,
A must.
Intelligence was our weapon of mass destruction.
Inside and out.

I am.....

Competent though starkly aware of my inadequacies
Breeding ground for cultural independence.
Opiates beware.
There is no place for you in this jungle.
Taking care of my own.
Each one, teach one.

I will always ....

Continue to fortify
The regions of my territory
Reaching back to pull others forward,
Be a black man who matters.
A panther.

S. Hafer Bronson

Muse(ic)

The rhythm of thoughts becoming words, becoming verses, ending in melodies.

S. Hafer Bronson

Theme from Taxi

It is odd how a simple melody or tune
Can make memories vividly
Reproduce into thoughts.
It can cause feelings
And emotions long buried to resurrect
Within your heart and overpower the "now".

Maybe it is the way for our subconscious
To connect past events to the present.
Maybe it is a defense mechanism that
Propels us into a time warp
As a means of escape from life's worries.
But no matter how painful the memory,
It is remembered with fondness and tenderness
Because we lived it
And we made it through.

The Music Lesson

This is a selfish thing I do.
Secret moments in careless pursuit
Of fulfillment.
No one can give this to me.
I must participate in the realization
Of this I seek.

Seemingly endless thoughts in preparation,
Calculated strategies,
Fantasy heaped upon fantasy,
Reality obscured, obsession mounting
Until the symphony is tuned
And begins to play.
I must listen carefully.
It is critical to my response.

Finely-tuned instruments
Producing such beauty through the senses,
The high, the low,
Forte, picicato,
Heightening expectations of
What is to come,
How it will finish.

The coda extends,
The senses rejoice once more
Into a fade.
No more bridges.

S. Hafer Bronson

Ode to a "Q"

Oh my! How you love me!
You call to me when your desires
Know no bounds.
You lead me into your sanctuary
To find contentment and peace.
(You are such a restless soul!)
You become the object of my desire
¡Mi amor! ¡Mi Corazon!
I bare my heart and soul and body
To you as I search to give you pleasure.

You wait.

I read your soul.
I feel your eyes.
I live your pain.
I find your joy.
I take it as my own!

My desire for oneness
Leaves you with shame, regret and sorrow.

You wait....

For me to leave.

Go Find You a Woman

(Cause I sure as hell done found me a man)

Been listening to your stories
Of attractions gone bad.
She always bypassed
The best thing she ever had.

I hate to say it but I've heard it all before.
They come into your life then right back out the door.

It's time to stop thinking about the "you" that is so fine
You're pushing sixty, babe; you're running out of time.
Get over yourself. Try taking a chance.
Accept her, love her, she might just understand.

I wonder how long it will take for you to see,
That life is short and love can set you free.
I used to be that way but now I understand,
Go find you a woman,
Cause I sure as hell done found me a man.

My lonely nights are gone.
My face is pimple free.
I learned to live and love.
I found ecstasy.
If you're wondering why this smile is tattooed on my face,
Just like Dick Tracy, he's always on the case.

And then I look at you and realize
You won't admit you're wrong, no compromise.
It has to be your way or the highway calls.
Control is everything or nothing at all.
Good luck my brother, I've tried to advise
But I've changed my focus. I've gotten wise.

I wonder how long it will take for you to see
That life is short and love can set you free.
I used to be that way but now I understand
Go find you a woman
Cause I sure as hell done found me a man.

(Bridge)
Stop picking her apart.
Stop rattling her chain.
What will you lose?
What can you gain?
What will convince you
That attraction is a two-way street?
If you don't let go and give in
You can't compete.

So what if her hair is short
And her hips a bit too wide?
You're still wearing a part in your hair
From Nineteen sixty-five!
It's time for you to see a new point of view.
Nobody's perfect, not even you!

I wonder how long it will take for you to see
That life is short and love can set you free.
I used to be that way but now I understand
Go find you a woman
Cause I sure as hell done found me a man.

Today I Bought a Pickup Truck

Today I bought a pickup truck
A Ford Ranger XLT.
It might not seem like much to you
But let me tell you, it set me free.
From promises gone unfulfilled
By family and friends.
But most of all my pickup truck
Replaces sorry-ass men.

Let me tell you about my Randy,
As it's affectionately known.
With a stick in the floor and a four-by-four,
He will always drive me home.

Music from the CD
Playing in my ears
And mirrors all around,
I get to watch his every move
As we bounce up and down.

I don't mean to badmouth Chevys
Dakotas or the Ram,
But I tell you they can't satisfy
Quite like my Randy can.

The truck bed is real handy
For things that I must do.
It's lined and has a cover
To camouflage the view.

He's got headlights to see
Where he ought to be.
Late at night when we're going fast,
With horses in his engine,
And a body that's built to last.

I don't mean to badmouth Chevys,
Dakotas or the Ram,
But I tell you they can't satisfy
Quite like my Randy can.

The rush my Randy gives me,
It cannot be denied.
When I start up his engine,
He keeps me satisfied.
A smooth and shiny finish
And a gate to block his tail.
An airbag for protection,
His cologne that new-truck smell.

I don't mean to badmouth Chevys
Dakotas or the Ram.
But I tell you they can't satisfy
Quite like my Randy can.

I don't wanna drive a Nissan.
I don't care about the P'up.
If they're made elsewhere
They don't compare
To my brand-new Ford truck.

(*Bridge*)
Sonoma, no Tacoma,
Can replace my XLT.
He drives me to work,
He drives me to church,
Then he drives me to ecstasy.
Made in America, built with pride,
Quality job one.
If I'm off to the mall
Or got things to haul,
My Randy gets it done.

But in time, he'll start to sputter,
To choke and even stall.
His body will rust from the mud and dust
That coat the underside.
And when he starts to break down
And I can't trust him anymore,
I can sell him in the classifieds
Then go by another Ford.

I don't mean to badmouth Chevys
I don't mean to buck the Ram.
But satisfaction's guaranteed,
So I don't give a damn.
 It sets me free from promises
From family and friends.
But best of all, my new Ford truck,
Replaces sorry-ass men.

S. Hafer Bronson

A Pledge of Love

For so long in my life, I have walked all alone,
As I waited to discover someone of my own
Who would love and accept unconditionally.
I want to know, will you marry me?

I fell into you with my heart and my soul.
And with you in my life, I know I am whole.
I want you with me for the rest my life.
Yes, my sweet love, I will be your wife.

On this day of promises, I will commit to you.
I pledge all my love. That's the best I can do.
And with this love, in love we will be
I want to know, will you marry me?

Our moments of solitude, our field of dreams,
Those walks through the park or fishing in the stream.
Those memories have created a void in my soul.
When we are apart, my mind loses control.

Will you marry me? Make my dream come true.
I am out of the forest, now that I've found you.
Will you marry me? My sweet gift from above.
I thank God for the presence of His grace
And our love.

My Momma Riding Shotgun

This is the story of a single mother with her One, One.
She is the greatest mother.
There ain't no other under the sun, sun.
We been riding together since the day that I was four-oh.
She kept it real, she kept it safe; she is my role, role.

My Ma, she chose to love and raised me through adoption.
My pop is gone but she rode strong and she my number one.
She cried, she sacrificed and raised me to a man, man.
Now I keep in touch and do things with her because I can, can.

I know she gets lonely; she don't complain but I can see it.
So I roll by her crib and take a peep and do
The son thang for a bit.

One day as I was leaving I said: Ma, you wanna ride, ride?
She say "cool," so I loaded her up,
Let back her seat and she confide, fide.

Ride me til I sweat. I must confess, I love the chauffeuring.
No keys to jangle, no rage to fight with horns a honking.
But I'm your momma so just to let you know,
I got your back, Stink.

We blood, real homies, no chicks and then she gave a wink, wink.
Then she changed the station,
Turned down the volume on my radio, oh.

What could I do? What could I say?
This is my momma,
I couldn't say "Hell no."
Hip hop was dropped for that ole school clock.
And I just shook my head.
I knew better than to try to change it
'Cause I'd be found stone cold dead.

So I made a sigh and enjoyed the ride
As I cruised the neighborhood.
Looked to my front, my back, left side and
Smiled cause it was all good.

Rolled up on some tooties wanting to
Fix me up with them booty bun, buns.
But, ain't gonna happen.
Cause to my right,
My Momma riding shotgun.
Yeah.
My momma riding shotgun.

My rap was cancelled by Emotions, Cocker,
And Marvin Gaye, Gaye.
Sexual Healing playing on the radio,
Mom began to sway, sway.
Window down, she was singing loud and
Drawing stares at every red light.

When the light would change,
I'd hit the gas then speed fast out of sight, sight.
But she's my Moms, no doubt that
She's a lot of fun, fun.
But I might have to recalculate
My momma riding shotgun.

About the Author

S. Hafer Bronson was born and raised in Charlotte, NC. From the age of eight until high school graduation, she attended parochial schools along with her two brothers.

She is an honors graduate with a Bachelor of Arts degree from North Carolina Central University. She also received a Masters of Education degree from University of North Carolina at Charlotte.

She worked for many years in the field of education before retiring in 2008.

She has been writing poetry for over twenty-five years. Her poetry is a reflection of her life experiences and observations on relationships, growth and sensuality.

S. Hafer is a member of Alpha Kappa Alpha Sorority, Inc. She currently lives in Concord, North Carolina with her husband, Arthur.

Made in the USA
San Bernardino, CA
29 April 2016